Cornerstones of Freedom

The Story of

Christopher Columbus

NICK ALFONSO

R. Conrad Stein

CHILDRENS PRESS®

CHICAGO

Library of Congress Cataloging-in-Publication Data

Stein, R. Conrad.
    Christopher Columbus / by R. Conrad Stein.

    p.   cm. — (Cornerstones of freedom)
    Summary: Describes the voyages and discoveries of
Columbus and their aftermath.
    ISBN 0-516-04851-1
    1. Columbus, Christopher—Juvenile literature.
2. Explorers—America—Biography—Juvenile literature.
3. Explorers—Spain—Biography—Juvenile literature.
4. America—Discovery and exploration—Spanish—
Juvenile literature. [1. Columbus, Christopher.
2. Explorers. 3. America—Discovery and exploration—
Spanish.] I. Title. II. Series.
E111.S85   1992
970.01'5'092—dc20
[B]   91-34744
                                      CIP
                                      AC

It was the late 1400s. For many years, the mysterious and wealthy lands of the East had lured Europeans. The Europeans called these lands the Indies, a term that included the East Indies, China, India, and Japan. Only a few bold travelers, such as Marco Polo, had been to the Indies. They brought back astonishing reports. Polo claimed that he had seen a ruby "the thickness of a man's arm, glowing like fire," and "all the precious spices that can be found in the world."

Marco Polo had journeyed to the Indies by a long, difficult route that went mostly over land. European merchants hoped to find a sea route to

Marco Polo traveled from Europe to Asia over land in the late 1200s.

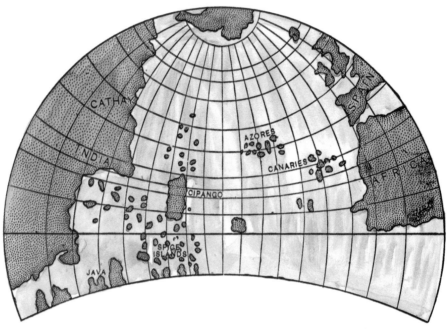

As this old map shows, before 1492, Europeans had no idea that the huge landmass of America lay between Europe and Asia.

the wealthy region. Christopher Columbus believed he could reach the East by sailing west. His desire to make the westward journey dominated his life.

The notion that one could find the Indies by sailing west was not held by Columbus alone. Most educated Europeans believed that the world was shaped like a ball. These educated people thought, however, that the lands of the East were simply too far away to be reached by sailing ships. In Columbus's time, such a voyage could be compared to how people in the 1930s viewed the idea of flying to the moon—as something that was feasible, but technically impossible.

Columbus dismissed the doubts and fears of others. A deeply religious man, he believed that

The Italian city of Genoa, where Christopher Columbus was born

God commanded him to find a new route to the Indies. Perhaps he also believed that God's direction over him began when, as a small boy, he developed a love for the sea.

Christopher Columbus was born in 1451 in the Italian city of Genoa. His father was a weaver who owned a small shop. At the time, Genoa was a lively seaport whose waterfront was a magnet for sailors. While growing up, young Christopher must have heard hundreds of sea stories. As an adult, he wrote, "At a very tender age I entered upon the sea sailing." Some of his biographers conclude that he took his first sea voyage when he was only ten years old.

The Lisbon harbor as it looked during Columbus's time

Serving on ships as a common sailor, Columbus worked his way up from deckhand to the rank of captain. He participated in many perilous voyages, including one to the frozen seas off Iceland and another to the Azores, far out into the forbidding Atlantic. When he was twenty-five, he worked on a Flemish merchant ship that was attacked and sunk by pirates. Wounded and hanging desperately onto an oar, Columbus swam six miles through treacherous waters to the shore. Oddly, the shipwreck proved to be a stroke of fortune. He had washed ashore near Lisbon, Portugal, one of the world's leading maritime centers.

For decades, Portuguese sailors had probed the seaways, hoping to find a route to the Indies. Years earlier, a powerful Portuguese prince, Henry the Navigator, had sent sea captains edging south along the African coast in hopes that they would sail around that continent and trade for the spices of the East. So far, Portuguese seamen had failed to find the Indies, but their ships had penetrated to the farthest edges of the known world. While living in Portugal, Columbus developed his idea of sailing west over the Atlantic in order to arrive at the spice-rich Eastern ports. Bringing back a cargo of expensive spices would earn vast riches for the sea captain.

The westward voyage Columbus wished to make would be enormously expensive. Seeking

Prince Henry the Navigator

Columbus in his study planning his voyage to the Indies

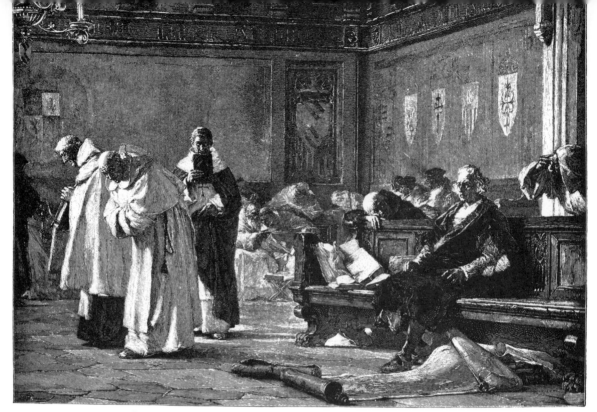

Columbus was laughed at by a commission of Spanish scholars when he presented his plan to reach the Indies by sailing westward.

Bartholomew Columbus

financing, he approached various kings and queens. Columbus was perhaps the finest seaman in all of Europe, and the monarchs listened to his proposal. King John II of Portugal rejected Columbus's idea because his nation was still committed to reaching the Indies by sailing around the African continent. Columbus's brother, Bartholomew, tried to obtain money from the kings of England and France, but neither monarch showed interest. Finally, Christopher Columbus turned to Ferdinand and Isabella, the king and queen of Spain.

At the time, Spain was emerging from a long and bloody war with the Moors of Granada.

Columbus explaining his plans to King Ferdinand and Queen Isabella

With final victory over the Moors approaching, the Spanish monarchs hoped to expand their power abroad. After much debate, they decided to give Columbus the money he needed to make the voyage. Queen Isabella became so enthusiastic about the project that she offered to pawn the crown jewels, if necessary, to finance the Columbus expedition.

An excited Christopher Columbus selected three ships to make the voyage—the *Pinta*, the *Niña*, and the *Santa María*. These were tiny vessels, none of them more than ninety feet long.

This sixteenth-century engraving shows Columbus saying farewell to Ferdinand and Isabella before departing on his voyage.

The banner of the expedition

Finding a crew was an even more daunting task than picking the ships. Few men were willing to venture out into the unknown regions of the Atlantic Ocean. Sailors called the frightening Atlantic the "Sea of Darkness." To give his project greater appeal, Columbus offered a small fortune to the first man who sighted land in the Indies. Lured by the money, a crew of ninety men was assembled to serve the three ships.

On August 3, 1492, the fleet set sail from Palos, Spain. Nine days later, the three ships docked at the Canary Islands to take on supplies and make repairs. On September 9, they left the islands— and the last-known land—behind them. Ahead

In Columbus's time, the unknown regions of the vast Atlantic Ocean were thought to contain all sorts of horrible dangers.

lay a vast, mysterious ocean which, the crew believed, had never been crossed before.

In those days, seamen rarely sailed out of sight of land. All of Columbus's men had heard terrifying stories about the hazards they would encounter in the middle of the Atlantic. According to one tale, the Atlantic was pockmarked by gigantic whirlpools so powerful they could suck the largest ships into the ocean depths. Another story told of ship-eating sea serpents that wrapped around a vessel and

The Niña, *the* Pinta, *and the* Santa María *on the open sea*

dragged it to the bottom. Still, the men did their duty and followed their captain. He believed that the power of God would deliver them to their destination.

"I have a favorable current . . . everyone is cheerful," wrote Columbus in his log after his first full week on the open sea. But despite this optimistic journal entry, it was clear that Columbus was worried about the faithfulness of his crew. Each day he lied to the men about the ships' progress, saying it was slower than its actual pace. Columbus had estimated that his fleet must sail 2,400 nautical miles before sighting land. He feared that if they traveled a greater distance than his estimate and still did not encounter land, the crew might mutiny. As he wrote in one long entry, "Today I made 180 miles . . . I recorded only 144 miles in order not to alarm the sailors if the voyage is lengthy."

Luck sailed with Columbus as he made his way west. By chance, he had entered into the westward trade winds, which would propel sailing ships across the Atlantic for centuries to come. But even these favorable winds upset the sailors. Every day, the mighty wind currents blew them deeper and deeper into the Atlantic. What if there was no land beyond the unknown reaches of this sea? How could they ever recross the ocean against such powerful winds?

Tensions rose among the crew after the third week in open waters. By now, they had been out of sight of land for longer than any other known crew in the history of seafaring. The sailors' intense desire to spot land played tricks with their minds. A cluster of low-hanging clouds looked to them like a mountainous island. A faint star flickering near the horizon took on the appearance of a distant campfire. One late afternoon, an officer on the bow of the *Pinta* shouted, "Land! Land!" The men on all three ships fell to their knees and offered a prayer of thanksgiving. But the morning sun revealed only

Pinta crew member Martín Alonso Pinzón mistakes clouds for land.

an empty ocean. The "land" the officer had seen proved to have been a low cloud formation.

Fearing certain death, the men plotted to murder Columbus, take over the vessels, and return to Spain. Only a passionate speech delivered by Columbus prevented mutiny. After the speech, one of the officers shouted, *"Adelante! Adelante!"* (Onward! Onward!), and the expedition continued.

In early October, signs of land appeared. The men saw logs and sticks floating on the surface of the water. In the sky were great flocks of birds. Still, as they looked anxiously at the horizon, the sailors saw no evidence of land itself. Then, on the night of October 11, Columbus noted an odd

sight. "About ten o'clock at night," he wrote in his log, "I thought I saw a light to the west. It looked like a little wax candle bobbing up and down." Could it finally be land? Columbus dismissed the thought. "I am first to admit that I was so eager to find land that I did not trust my own senses."

Bright moonlight shone over the waters during the early-morning hours of October 12, 1492. At about 2:00 A.M., a sailor aboard the *Pinta* sighted a shoreline and hurried to tell his captain. The captain fired the deck cannon to alert the other ships. As dawn came, the rising

Columbus and his crew rejoicing at the sight of land

This 1493 woodcut is the earliest pictorial version of Columbus's landing in America.

sun revealed an island that was part of the chain now known as the Bahamas. After thirty-six frightening days on the open sea, the men rejoiced at the sight.

In a small boat, Columbus and his officers rowed to the beach. There he claimed the island for Spain, naming it San Salvador. "No sooner had we concluded the formalities of taking possession of the island," wrote Columbus, "than people began to come to the beach, all as naked as their mothers bore them." These were the Arawak, a people who were native to the islands. Columbus, believing he was in the Indies, mistakenly called them "Indians." It was because

A present-day photograph of the island in the Bahamas where Columbus is thought to have first landed

of this blunder that the native inhabitants of the Americas were ever after referred to as "Indians" in most European languages.

As grateful as he was to find land, Columbus must have felt a wave of disappointment. Where were the great cities of the Indies? Where were the traders ready to supply the ships with tasty spices and fragrant perfumes? Where were the powerful rulers of the East who, as Marco Polo had claimed, lived in golden palaces?

Columbus had no idea that during those dangerous days and nights on the Atlantic he had been relentlessly pursuing a goal that was based on two huge miscalculations. First, he had grossly underestimated the size of the earth. East Asia lay about 11,000 nautical miles from the Canary Islands, not the mere 2,400 that he had calculated. His second mistake was to assume that the westward passage to the Indies would be made up mostly of open sea. He had not imagined—nor could any European—that the huge continents of North and South America barred the way to the East.

Convinced that the land of spices lay nearby, Columbus sailed away from the Bahamas to seek more promising territory. He found a maze of islands and stopped to explore many of them. On Cuba, which he mistook for Japan, he found the native people "drinking the smoke" of a curious

A map showing the route of Columbus's first voyage

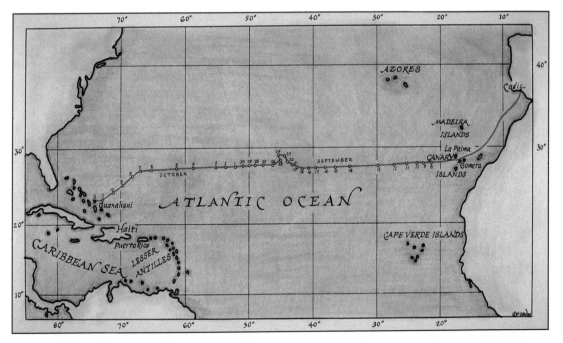

On December 24, the Santa María *was wrecked off the coast of an island the Spaniards came to call Hispaniola.*

plant they called *tobacos*. On present-day Haiti, he was moved by such profound beauty that "a thousand tongues would not suffice [to describe it]." About the tropical waters, he wrote, "Here the fishes are so unlike ours that it is amazing. . . . [Their colors] are so bright that anyone would marvel and take a great delight at seeing them."

All these wonders, but where were the riches of the East?

On Christmas Eve, 1492, the *Santa María* was wrecked off an island the Spaniards came to call Hispaniola. Today this island is shared by the

The native people of Hispaniola helped Columbus's shipwrecked crew.

nations of Haiti and the Dominican Republic. Columbus decided to build a fortress out of the *Santa María*'s boards, and leave about forty men on Hispaniola while he returned to Spain for supplies. Despite the shipwreck, Columbus was in high spirits. The local chief was so friendly that he ordered his own people to help build the fort, which was named La Navidad. Columbus also noticed that the chief owned several golden ornaments. Even if there proved to be no spices in this land, perhaps the Europeans would find gold—an even more precious commodity.

The return voyage was a sea captain's nightmare. Far into the Atlantic, a storm struck, and the *Pinta* and the *Niña* lost sight of each other. So violent was the storm that Columbus, aboard the *Pinta*, believed that his ship was lost. Hastily, he wrote an account of his discoveries, placed the account in a waterproof keg, and threw the keg overboard. That way, he reasoned, someone might find the keg and learn the fate of his expedition. But after days of towering waves,

Fearing that his ship was lost, Columbus placed the ship's log in a waterproof keg and threw it overboard.

As this highly romanticized painting shows, Columbus was given a hero's welcome by King Ferdinand and Queen Isabella.

the weather cleared, and both the *Pinta* and the *Niña* reached Palos, Spain, on March 15, 1492.

At the court of Ferdinand and Isabella, Columbus was given a hero's welcome. The king and queen looked in awe at the foreign-looking "Indians" Columbus had captured and taken with him. In gratitude, the Spanish monarchs gave Columbus the title Admiral of the Ocean Sea, and agreed to finance another voyage. Ferdinand and Isabella also named Columbus governor of all future colonies he might establish in the lands across the waters.

Columbus finds the bodies of some of his slain men at La Navidad.

On September 25, 1493, Columbus set sail again. This time he commanded a fleet of seventeen ships and about a thousand men. Columbus had been ordered to establish a colony in the new lands. The fleet made excellent time on this second voyage, spotting land in just twenty-one sailing days.

When he arrived at his fort on the island of Hispaniola, Columbus discovered a disaster. All of the men he had left there had been killed by angry islanders. Columbus questioned the fearful native islanders and heard a tragic story. The Spaniards, in their zeal to find gold, had tortured and brutalized the native people. The islanders rebelled and slaughtered the Europeans. The massacre on Hispaniola was the first—but certainly not the last—large-scale episode of warfare between Europeans and Native Americans.

During his second voyage, Columbus explored the southern coast of Cuba, as well as Jamaica and Puerto Rico. He established a second colony on Hispaniola, but this one also was beset by troubles. The men who had come on this voyage were gold-seeking adventurers, not colonists. Dissatisfied with the small amount of gold they found on Hispaniola, they fought with the native people and among themselves. Several of the rebel colonists sailed back to Spain, where they spread rumors that Columbus was a corrupt and incompetent governor. Columbus, once a hero in the hearts of Spaniards, now became viewed as a scoundrel.

Isabela, the second colony established by Columbus on Hispaniola

Columbus returned from his second voyage in June 1496. This time, no hero's welcome awaited him in Spain. He had failed to meet the grand leaders of Asia. The ships' holds contained no valuable spices, and Columbus's ability to govern the new lands was in question.

Still, the king and queen of Spain sent Columbus on a third voyage. He departed from

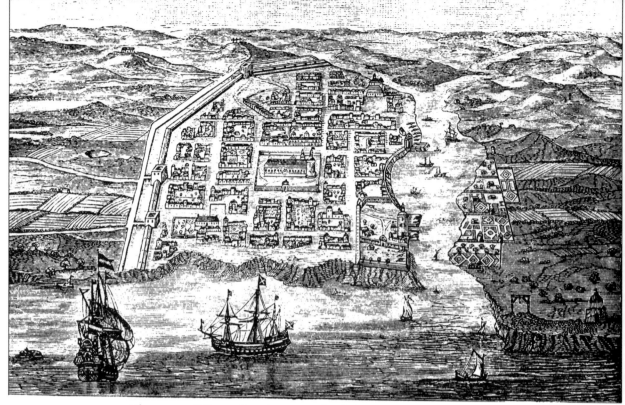

The town of Santo Domingo was built by Spanish colonists after Columbus's second trip to Hispaniola.

Spain on May 30, 1498. On his prior trips he had encountered only islands. During this journey, he stepped upon the shores of the South American continent at present-day Venezuela. In a mystical mood, he wrote that Venezuela's Orinoco River led to the Garden of Eden, "the earthly paradise, which no one can reach except by the will of God."

Certainly no paradise was the colony at Hispaniola, where Columbus arrived in August 1498. The native population there was fast dying off because the Spaniards had killed thousands and forced the remainder into brutal slavery in the goldfields. Also, the Spanish colonists continued to fight with each other. A new

Spanish governor arrived in Hispaniola in 1500 and promptly arrested Columbus for fostering disorder in the colony. The governor sent Columbus back to Spain in chains to stand trial.

In Spain, Ferdinand and Isabella declared Columbus not guilty of any wrongdoing in the colony. They even sent him on a fourth voyage, though some historians claim that by this time, the king and queen simply wanted to get rid of the aging sea captain.

The fourth voyage proved to be the most trying one for the admiral. In the Caribbean Sea, a terrible storm tossed his fleet of four vessels about as if they were toy boats in a bathtub. "I

During his third visit to Hispaniola, Columbus was arrested by the Spanish colonial governor and sent back to Spain in chains.

During the fourth voyage to America, Columbus and his men endured terrible storms.

was never without . . . wind, water, and cloudbursts," he wrote, "so that the end of the world seemed to have come." The storm caused sea water to seep into the ship's cargo, and the food onboard soon became infested with insects. Sailors were forced to wait until dark to eat so that they would not see the maggots crawling in their bread.

Near the island of Jamaica, Columbus abandoned ship. He and his men became marooned on that island for a year. They all would have starved had not Columbus tricked Jamaica's native people into feeding them. He told the islanders that he would command a powerful god to rise into the sky and eat up the

The people of Jamaica gave Columbus food after he tricked them into believing that he had made God blot out the moon.

moon. Actually, he had read in his almanac that an eclipse would blot out a portion of the moon on the night of February 29, 1504. When the moon did appear to be devoured in the night sky, the panicky islanders gave Columbus and his men all the food they needed.

Columbus returned to Spain in November 1504, and his career as an explorer came to an end. He now suffered from crippling arthritis that made his every step painful. Still, he hoped that the Spanish king would reappoint him governor of the colonies in the new lands. The king refused even to speak to the once-exalted Admiral of the Ocean Sea.

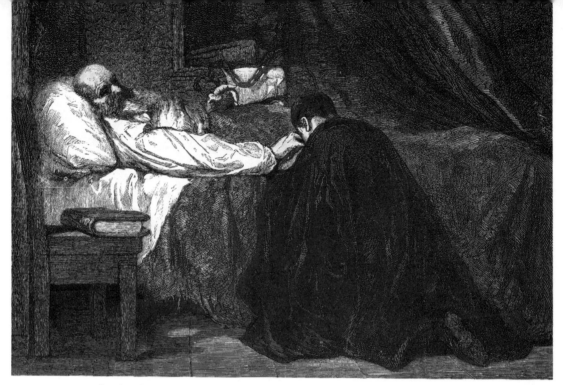

The death of Columbus

Christopher Columbus died on May 20, 1506, in Valladolid, Spain. At the time of his death, he still believed that the spice-rich Indies lay somewhere near the lands he had discovered.

Today—some five hundred years after his first voyage—Columbus remains a towering figure in history. However, he did not, as American schoolchildren were once taught, "discover America." Ancestors of the people we call Native Americans trekked from Asia to the Americas thousands of years before Columbus's time. And recent findings made by archaeologists confirm that Norsemen settled in Newfoundland around A.D. 1000. Some historians believe that the huge American landmass had other visitors before Columbus—Africans, Chinese, Irish monks,

French fishermen. Still, it was Columbus's voyage that opened the door to the Americas and triggered a mass migration from the Old World to the New World. His journeys certainly made him one of the greatest explorers of all time.

Shortly after Columbus's death, an interesting biography was written about him by his son Ferdinand. Ferdinand claimed that his father had been an avid reader of the Roman philosopher Seneca. Columbus's favorite line from Seneca had been, "A time will come when the chains of the Ocean will fall apart, and a vast continent be revealed." As Ferdinand wrote, "This prophecy was fulfilled by my father the Admiral, in the year 1492."

Columbus departing from Spain on his first voyage to the New World

INDEX

PHOTO CREDITS

Cover, SuperStock; 1, Historical Pictures Service, Chicago; 2, SuperStock; 3, Historical Pictures Service, Chicago; 4, 5, 6, 7 (both pictures), 8 (both pictures), North Wind; 9, Historical Pictures Service, Chicago; 10 (both pictures), 11, North Wind; 12, SuperStock; 13, 14, North Wind; 15, 16, 17, Historical Pictures Service, Chicago; 18, © Cameramann International, Ltd.; 19, 20, Historical Pictures Service, Chicago; 21, 22, North Wind; 23, SuperStock; 24, 25, 26, 27, 28, 29, 30, North Wind; 31, SuperStock

Picture Identifications:
Cover: Columbus departing from Hispaniola
Page 1: The first sighting of land by Columbus
Page 2: Columbus arriving at the monastery of La Rábida in 1485; it was there that his son, Diego, stayed while Columbus traveled about to find support for his proposed explorations

Project Editor: Shari Joffe
Designer: Karen Yops
Cornerstones of Freedom Logo: David Cunningham

ABOUT THE AUTHOR

R. Conrad Stein was born and raised in Chicago. He enlisted in the Marine Corps at the age of eighteen and served for three years. He then attended the University of Illinois, where he received a bachelor's degree in history. He later studied in Mexico, earning an advanced degree from the University of Guanajuato. Mr. Stein is the author of many books, articles, and short stories for young people.

Mr. Stein lives in Chicago with his wife and their daughter Janna.